I DONUT DARE YOU!

Bold Breakfast–Inspired Desserts for Anytime

by HEATHER KIM

COMPASS POINT BOOKS
a capstone imprint

Cap'n Crunch®
Monster Cookies
10

Black Tea Shortbread
12

Pumpkin Spice Latte Balls
with Chex Mix® Crumble
16

Chocolate Latte
Semifreddo with
Chocolate Coffee Beans
20

Cannoli Waffles
24

Five-Spice Donut Muffins
with Coconut Dip
28

Chocolate Bagel Pudding
with Cream Cheese
Ice Cream
34

Crumby Coffee Cake
40

Cinnamon Rolls with
Honey Glaze
42

Mochi Donuts with
Lemon Nutmeg Glaze
and Coffee Dip   18

Streusel Strudel   32

Milk Bread Rolls and
Next-Day Griddle Toast   44

TABLE OF CONTENTS

BREAKFAST FOR DESSERT

Nothing screams dessert like the smell of freshly baked crumb cakes, donuts, or strudel cooling in the kitchen. A great-tasting dessert adds a delicious touch to almost any meal—even breakfast!

But these aren't your average early morning treats. Here you'll find daring dessert recipes that are easy to make and even easier to enjoy. Take a traditional favorite like chocolate chip cookies and add Cap'N Crunch® cereal. Experiment with crowd-pleasers such as coffee cake by adding a yummy streusel topping. Or combine a breakfast go-to—bagels!—with classic desserts like pudding and ice cream.

Is your mouth watering yet? Gather your ingredients, whip up these bold breakfast-inspired treats, and share them with family and friends anytime of day.

PLAYING IT SAFE

Cooking and baking are fun, especially when you're trying new recipes. Make sure to stay safe too by remembering a few basic kitchen safety tips.

Always wash your hands before you begin, if you spill, and after touching raw eggs.

Be careful when handling sharp objects. Ask for an adult's help when a recipe calls for chopping, slicing, or cutting. Hold the knife's handle firmly when cutting. Keep fingers away from the blade.

Use caution when working near hot surfaces. When using saucepans, turn the handles toward the center of the stove to avoid bumping a handle and spilling. Have an adult help when operating the stovetop and oven. Always wear oven mitts or pot holders to take hot baking sheets or cake pans out of the oven.

Spills and messes are bound to happen. Wipe up spills with paper towels or a damp kitchen towel right away. Keep your countertop clean and dry.

MIX IT UP

Read through each recipe before you begin. Make sure you have all the right supplies. Some recipes require several hours before they are ready, so plan ahead. If you're not sure how to perform one of the techniques required, check this handy guide.

mixing bowl

stand mixer

mixing spoon

beater

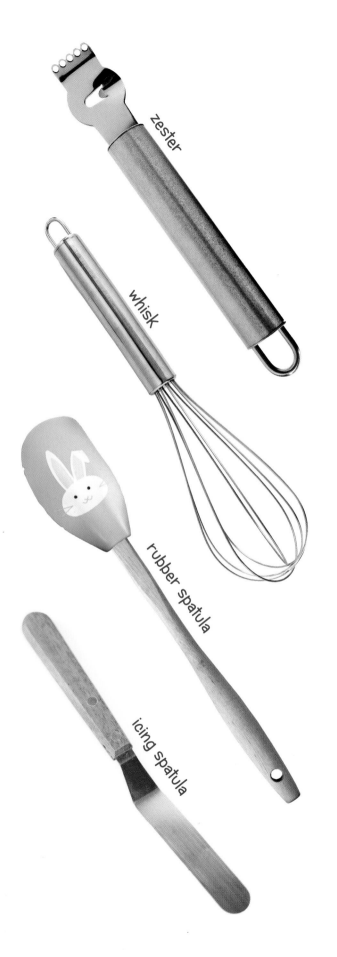

zester

whisk

rubber spatula

icing spatula

BEAT IT

Create a smooth, creamy mixture by stirring briskly, using a spoon, whisk, or mixer.

CREAM IT

Vigorously beat and stir ingredients. The result? Creamy, fluffy smoothness.

GREASE IT

To grease a pan, use a stick of butter to thinly coat the inside of the pan. If you don't have butter, you can use cooking spray.

KNEAD IT

Move dough to a clean workspace lightly dusted with flour. Press into the dough with the palm of your hand, pushing it away from you. Repeat until the dough is smooth.

WHISK IT

Use a whisk to combine ingredients using a side-to-side motion. If you don't have a whisk, use two forks.

WHIP IT

Add air and volume to a mixture using a whisk or mixer.

ZEST IT

Shred tiny bits of the outer, colorful rind or peel of a citrus fruit to add fresh flavor to the recipe.

COOKIE CRAVINGS

Is there anything more irresistible than a warm, ooey-gooey cookie fresh out of the oven? If they're breakfast-inspired cookies, then, yes!

CAP'N CRUNCH® MONSTER COOKIES

Cereal—it's not just for breakfast! It's also for cookies. Combine it with chocolate chips, M&M's®, oats, and graham cracker crumbs to make monster cookies. Come on, now. These monsters are nothing to be afraid of.

INGREDIENTS

1 cup butter, room temp

1 cup granulated sugar

2/3 cup brown sugar

1 tablespoon corn syrup

1 egg

1 tablespoon heavy cream

1 teaspoon vanilla extract

1 2/3 cups all-purpose flour

1/2 teaspoon baking powder

1/4 teaspoon baking soda

1 tablespoon salt

2/3 cup mini chocolate chips

1 cup M&M's® chocolate candies

2/3 cup graham cracker crumbs

2/3 cup old-fashioned oats

2/3 cup cornmeal

1 tablespoon milk powder

4 snack-size bags Nacho Cheese Doritos®

1 cup Cap'n Crunch®

– SASSY TIP –
Chill cookie dough in the fridge for up to 24 hours before baking. Chilling the dough helps concentrate the flavor.

SASSY FACT
Made for nonstick cooking, a Silpat® silicone rubber mat is great when working with sticky stuff, like gooey batter, taffy, caramel, or dough.

1 Preheat oven to 375°F.

2 In a large bowl, use an electric mixer to combine the butter, both sugars, and corn syrup on medium speed for about 5 minutes.

3 Add the egg, heavy cream, and vanilla extract. Mix on medium speed for another 8 minutes or so.

4 In another bowl, stir together the remaining ingredients. Add them to the dough mixture. Mix everything on slow until just incorporated. Do not overmix.

5 Drop spoonfuls onto a parchment- or Silpat®-lined baking sheet, 2 inches (5 cm) apart. Bake for about 18 minutes, turning the sheet halfway through.

6 Remove from the oven when the cookies are golden. Let cool on the sheet for 1 minute. Then transfer cookies to a cooling rack. Let cool completely before serving.

BLACK TEA SHORTBREAD

Shortbread originated in Scotland during medieval times. Mary, Queen of Scots (1542–1587), had a special team of French chefs who perfected the shortbread recipe. With only a few ingredients, you won't have to travel far to enjoy this Scottish sweet treat!

INGREDIENTS

2 sticks butter, room temp

1/2 cup powdered sugar

2 teaspoons finely ground black tea

2 cups all-purpose flour

1 teaspoon vanilla extract

pinch of salt

1 Preheat oven to 350°F. Line a cookie sheet with a Silpat® mat or parchment paper.

2 In a large mixing bowl, cream the butter and sugar together until pale-golden and fluffy.

3 Add the tea, flour, and vanilla extract. Mix until well-combined.

4 Dust a clean surface with powdered sugar. Gently roll out dough to 0.5 inch (1 cm) thickness. Cut into squares or desired shapes.

5 Bake for 10 for 12 minutes or until just golden.

– SASSY TIP –
Not a fan of black tea? Substitute with a caffeine-free alternative, such as green, chamomile, or mint.

CAFFEINE FIX

Perk up any meal with these coffee-containing desserts. Not a caffeine person? You can make all of these recipes without the coffee.

PUMPKIN SPICE LATTE BALLS WITH CHEX MIX® CRUMBLE

Wake up! Theses deliciously spicy. caffeinated balls provide a punch of power along with a crunch. Pop one when you need a boost or make a batch for a sleepyhead friend.

CRUMBLE

1 teaspoon cinnamon

2 tablespoons granulated sugar

1 cup Chocolate Chex Mix®, crumbled

1 packet instant coffee

BALLS

2/3 cup coconut oil, room temp

1/2 cup granulated sugar

1/2 cup pumpkin pie filling

1/4 cup peanut butter

1 teaspoon vanilla extract

1/4 teaspoon salt

1 packet instant coffee

1 teaspoon cinnamon

3/4 cup coconut flour

1/2 cup sweet rice flour

fresh nutmeg, grated

1 Put all the Chex Mix® crumble ingredients into a gallon-sized, resealable plastic bag and shake. Set aside.

2 In a medium bowl, whip the coconut oil and sugar until fluffy and smooth.

3 Add the remaining ball ingredients and stir together until completely combined.

4 Scoop and shape dough into 1-inch (2.5-cm) truffle balls.

5 Place one or two truffle balls into the bag of Chex Mix® crumble. Gently shake the bag until balls are completely coated. Repeat with all balls.

6 Refrigerate balls for about 1 hour.

> **SASSY FACT**
> Nutmeg is a nut, right?
> WRONG. It's a seed from
> an evergreen tree.

MOCHI DONUTS WITH LEMON NUTMEG GLAZE AND COFFEE DIP

Donut miss out on this dessert! These homemade donuts will leave your kitchen smelling like a bakery. To eat, dunk in the coffee-flavored dip. It'll leave your taste buds buzzing and your stomach wanting more.

STARTER DOUGH

1/4 cup glutinous rice flour

3 tablespoons whole milk

DONUTS

1 3/4 cups sweet rice flour

1/2 cup whole milk

2 1/2 tablespoons unsalted butter, melted

1/4 cup granulated sugar

1 egg

1 teaspoon baking powder

4 cups neutral-tasting oil, for frying

GLAZE

2 1/2 tablespoons unsalted butter, melted

1 cup powdered sugar

1/2 teaspoon vanilla extract

1/2 teaspoon lemon peel

grated nutmeg (fresh, if possible), to taste

2 to 3 tablespoons hot water

1 Mix starter dough ingredients together in a microwave-safe bowl. Microwave for 30 seconds. Set aside to cool for about 5 minutes.

2 Meanwhile, combine donut ingredients (except the oil) in a large stand mixer bowl and combine with a dough hook. Add starter dough and continue mixing until totally combined. If you don't have a dough hook, knead the dough with your hands.

3 Dust a clean surface with rice flour. Roll out the dough to 0.5 inch (1 cm) thickness. Cut out donut shapes using a donut cutter or two concentric cutters.

4 Heat oil in a big pot over medium heat until it reaches 350°F on a candy thermometer. Drop in a few donuts and watch them sink and then float back up. Fry for a few minutes on each side until golden and fluffy. Use tongs to transfer donuts to a paper-towel-lined tray to drain grease.

5 For glaze, mix the butter, powdered sugar, vanilla extract, lemon, and nutmeg in a small bowl. Dilute with 2 to 3 tablespoons of hot water to desired consistency.

6 To assemble, dip one side of each donut into glaze.

COFFEE DIP

1 cup sweetened condensed milk

1/3 cup espresso (or strong instant coffee)

1/4 teaspoon almond extract

1/2 teaspoon vanilla extract

1/2 teaspoon salt

TO MAKE

Whisk all ingredients together in a small bowl until completely combined. Serve warm.

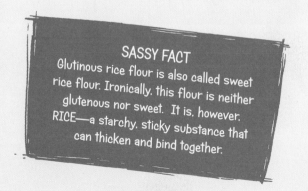

SASSY FACT
Glutinous rice flour is also called sweet rice flour. Ironically, this flour is neither glutenous nor sweet. It is, however, RICE—a starchy, sticky substance that can thicken and bind together.

CHOCOLATE LATTE SEMIFREDDO WITH CHOCOLATE COFFEE BEANS

This dessert combines three of the guiltiest pleasures—chocolate, coffee, and ice cream. *Semifreddo* is Italian for semi-frozen. And a *latte* is how much of this fabulous dessert you will want to eat.

SEMIFREDDO

3 tablespoons instant coffee

4 large eggs, separated

1 tablespoon vanilla extract

1/4 cup granulated sugar

1 1/4 cups heavy cream

4 ounces chocolate bar, finely chopped

1 Line a loaf pan with plastic wrap, leaving some overhanging on all sides.

2 In a medium bowl, mix the instant coffee, egg yolks, vanilla extract, and sugar. Beat with a whisk until thick.

3 In a separate medium bowl, beat the egg whites until stiff.

5 In another medium bowl, beat cream in a separate bowl until it holds its shape.

6 Fold the cream into the coffee mixture. Carefully add the egg whites and the chocolate bar pieces. Transfer the mixture to the loaf pan. Cover with the overhanging plastic wrap. Place in freezer for 2 hours.

7 To serve, turn upside down and pull off the plastic wrap. Release onto a platter and slice. Top with chocolate coffee beans.

CHOCOLATE COFFEE BEANS

2/3 cup semisweet chocolate chips

1 1/2 teaspoons vegetable shortening

1/2 cup coffee beans

1 In a small bowl, microwave chocolate chips and shortening until melted and smooth.

2 Dip the coffee beans in chocolate mixture and allow excess to drip off.

3 Place each bean on waxed paper. Let stand for 10 to 15 minutes or until firm.

> **– SASSY TIP –**
> To separate egg yolks from the whites, crack open the egg over a bowl. Let the whites fall into a bowl below. Move the yolk back and forth between the two halves of the cracked egg until all the white has fallen below. Save the whites for another use. Remember to always wash your hands with soap and water after touching raw eggs.

WITH CREAM, PLEASE

After a filling meal, there's nothing better than a rich, velvety-smooth dessert. These creamy, savory sweets will hit the spot—and are perfect for showcasing your baking skills!

CANNOLI WAFFLES

Italian dessert, meet Belgian breakfast. Sandwiched between these waffles is the same rich, creamy filling that's inside cannoli—a traditional Italian sweet. Topped with candied pistachios and chocolate coffee sauce, it's a completely perfect breakfast for dessert.

WAFFLES

2 cups all-purpose flour

1 tablespoon + 1 teaspoon baking powder

1/2 teaspoon salt

1/4 cup granulated sugar

2 eggs, separated (see page 21)

2 cups whole milk

1/2 teaspoon vanilla extract

1/2 cup vegetable oil

– SASSY TIP –
If you're short on time, use toaster waffles and just make the filling.

1 Mix all the dry ingredients together in a medium bowl. Set aside.

2 In another bowl, beat egg whites until fluffy and stiff.

3 In a separate large bowl, mix the egg yolks, milk, vanilla extract, and oil.

4 Add dry-ingredient mixture into the large bowl of wet ingredients. Mix well.

5 Gently fold in beaten egg whites, maintaining fluffiness.

6 Cook the waffle batter according to waffle-iron instructions.

FILLING

3/4 cup powdered sugar

1 teaspoon ground cinnamon

1 cup mascarpone cheese

1 cup ricotta cheese

1/4 cup heavy cream

1/4 cup small, semisweet chocolate chips

zest of 1 lemon

fresh nutmeg, grated

1 In a big bowl, whisk together the sugar, cinnamon, and mascarpone and ricotta cheeses until silky-smooth.

2 In a separate mixing bowl, beat the heavy cream until stiffened.

3 Using a rubber spatula, gently fold cream into ricotta mixture, maintaining fluffiness.

4 Stir in chocolate chips, lemon zest, and nutmeg. Refrigerate for 1 to 1.5 hours.

Recipe continues on next page.

CANDIED PISTACHIOS

1 cup granulated sugar

1 cup pistachios, shelled

salt, to taste

1 **Spread a single layer of pistachios onto a parchment- or Silpat®-lined baking sheet. Set aside.**

2 **On the stovetop, add an even layer of sugar to a nonstick saucepan or skillet. Melt sugar, continuously stirring with a rubber spatula, until golden-amber (not brown). If sugar burns, discard and try again!**

3 **Immediately pour melted sugar over pistachios. Sprinkle with salt.**

4 **Once cooled and hardened, break candied pistachios into tiny pieces. Place in a large, resealable plastic bag and crush.**

CHOCOLATE COFFEE SAUCE

1 cup semisweet mini chocolate chips

2 tablespoons corn syrup

1 cup heavy cream

1 packet (or 1 heaping teaspoon) instant coffee

pinch of salt

TO MAKE

On stovetop, mix all the ingredients in a medium saucepan over low heat. Whisk continuously until melted and totally incorporated.

TO ASSEMBLE

1 **Sandwich cold cannoli filling between two hot waffles.**

2 **Sprinkle with candied pistachios and drizzle chocolate coffee sauce on top.**

FIVE-SPICE DONUT MUFFINS WITH COCONUT DIP

Just can't get enough donuts? Then these muffins just might be the cure for your donut addiction. Nutmeg and cinnamon along with a spicy and sweet topping make these a comforting snack.

MUFFINS

3 cups all-purpose flour

1 tablespoon baking powder

1 teaspoon salt

1/2 teaspoon ground nutmeg

1/2 teaspoon cinnamon

1 cup granulated sugar

4 tablespoons butter, softened

2 large eggs

1/2 teaspoon vanilla extract

1 cup whole milk

1 Preheat oven to 350°F. Grease two 12-cup muffin tins.

2 In a large bowl, stir together the flour, baking powder, salt, nutmeg, and cinnamon.

3 In another bowl, cream together the sugar and butter. Add the eggs and vanilla extract and mix again.

4 Add the flour mixture and milk alternately to the creamed mixture, beating well and scraping the sides of bowl down after each addition.

5 Fill the prepared muffin pans about two-thirds full. Bake until golden, about 15 to 20 minutes.

Recipe continues on next page.

COCONUT DIP

3 large egg yolks (see page 21)

1/2 cup + 2 tablespoons granulated sugar

1/4 teaspoon salt

1 tablespoon cornstarch

1 cup coconut milk

1 teaspoon pandan extract

1 **In a medium saucepan, whisk together the yolks, sugar, salt, and cornstarch until smooth.**

2 **Pour in coconut milk and bring to a boil, whisking constantly. When mixture thickens to pudding (about 2 minutes), take off heat.**

3 **Stir in extract. Let cool.**

SASSY FACT

Also known as pandan essence or screw pine paste, pandan extract is a natural flavoring and colorant. It comes from the palm-like leaves of the pandan plant found in southeast Asia and the Hawaiian islands. Pandan has a nutty, vanilla-like flavor. You can find it at Asian markets, but vanilla extract works well as a substitute.

TOPPING

1 cup sugar

1 tablespoon five spice

1 tablespoon cocoa powder

1 stick butter, melted

1. Mix the sugar, five spice, and cocoa in a small bowl.

2. Coat muffins in melted butter. Immediately roll them in mixture.

3. Transfer to a cooling rack. Serve warm with coconut dip.

STREUSEL STRUDEL

Can you say "streusel strudel" ten times fast? Cream cheese and streusel fill this strudel. with more streusel sprinkled on top. If your tongue is twisted now, just wait until you taste it!

STREUSEL

1/3 cup granulated sugar

2 tablespoons all-purpose flour

2 tablespoons butter

1/2 teaspoon cinnamon

pinch of nutmeg (fresh, if possible)

TO MAKE

In a medium bowl, mix all ingredients together until crumbly. Set aside.

STRUDEL

1/2 package puff-pastry sheets, thawed

3 ounces cream cheese, softened

1/4 teaspoon cardamom or cinnamon

4 ounces bitter chocolate, chopped

1 Preheat oven to 400°F.

2 Unfold the pastry sheets on a lightly floured surface. Cut sheet in half to form two rectangles. Fold one rectangle in half the long way.

3 With a sharp knife, cut nine slits through the folded side to within 0.5 inch (1 cm) of the opposite edge.

4 In a small bowl, stir together cream cheese and cardamom or cinnamon.

5 Spread mixture to within 0.5 inch (1 cm) of the pastry edge. Sprinkle with chocolate and then sprinkle with half of the streusel.

6 Unfold the pastry and place it over the edge. Press edges to seal.

7 Sprinkle remaining half of the streusel on top of the pastry.

8 Bake for 15 minutes or until golden brown.

CHOCOLATE BAGEL PUDDING WITH CREAM CHEESE ICE CREAM

Turn yesterday's breakfast into today's dessert. Use leftover bagels to make chocolate pudding and top with homemade ice cream for a sweet, satisfying snack.

PUDDING

1 pound plain bagels (preferably day-old)

1 cup heavy cream

1 cup granulated sugar

1/4 cup cocoa powder

1/2 teaspoon salt

1 cup semisweet chocolate chips

1 cup dark chocolate chips

2 large eggs

2 large egg yolks (see page 21)

2 cups whole milk

1 tablespoon vanilla extract

1 teaspoon chocolate extract

– SASSY TIP –
To make a water bath, place your baking dish or muffin pan into a larger pan or rimmed baking sheet. Fill the outside pan with a small amount (a fingertip worth) of hot water and pop in the oven.

1. Dice bagels into small cubes (about 7 cups).

2. In a large stockpot, stir the heavy cream, sugar, cocoa powder, and salt until boiling.

3. Remove from heat and immediately add the semisweet and dark chocolate chips. Let stand for a couple minutes, then whisk until smooth.

4. In a medium bowl, whisk together eggs, egg yolks, milk, and extracts. Mix this combo into the chocolate, and then stir in bagel cubes, combining.

5. Cover mixture with plastic wrap, making sure the bread is completely covered in liquid. Refrigerate for 2 hours or overnight.

6. Preheat oven to 325°F.

7. Pour chocolate-bagel pudding mixture into a greased 8- by 8-inch (20- by 20-cm) baking dish or large muffin pans for bite-sized servings.

8. Bake in a water bath until completely set and slightly golden, about an hour for an 8- by 8-inch (20- by 20-cm) dish or 35 minutes for muffins. The centers should feel firm.

9. Let cool slightly. Serve while still warm.

Recipe continues on next page.

ICE CREAM

1 1/2 cups heavy cream

1 (8-ounce) package cream cheese, room temp

1 (14-ounce) can sweetened condensed milk

3/4 cup cherry pie filling

1 packet (or 1 heaping teaspoon) instant coffee

1/2 cup graham crackers, crushed

1. In a large mixing bowl, whip heavy cream until stiff peaks form. Scrape into a clean bowl. Set aside.

2. In the dirty mixing bowl, beat cream cheese until smooth. Add sweetened condensed milk and beat again until smooth.

3. Fold whipped cream into cream-cheese mixture. Be careful not to deflate the whipped cream.

4. Pour half of the cream mixture into a plastic-wrapped, 9- by 5-inch (23- by 13-cm) loaf pan. Drizzle with half of the cherry pie filling and sprinkle on half of the instant coffee and crushed graham crackers. Swirl together.

5. Add the remaining cream mixture. Top with the rest of the cherry pie filling, instant coffee, and crushed graham crackers. Swirl together.

6. Cover with plastic wrap and freeze until firm, about 4 hours.

7. Serve over warm chocolate bagel pudding.

– SASSY TIP –
How will you know when stiff peaks have formed? Lift your whisk out of the cream. Some cream will stick straight up on the whisk. If the cream falls back over, it's a soft peak and you need to keep whipping.

SWEET CAKES AND ROLLS

Ready for melt-in-your-mouth goodness? These divine, easy-to-make sweet cakes and rolls are best warm out of the oven. But you can also tuck them into a lunch box for a mid-morning snack or afternoon treat.

CRUMBY COFFEE CAKE

This coffee cake may be crumby, but it certainly isn't crummy! The streusel topping adds a complex layer of goodness. Then throw on some rainbow sprinkles for a colorful flair.

STREUSEL

1 box cake mix

1 teaspoon vanilla extract

1/3 cup oil

rainbow sprinkles, to taste

CAKE

1 1/2 cups all-purpose flour

1 cup granulated sugar

2 teaspoons baking powder

1/2 teaspoon baking soda

1/2 teaspoon salt

1 cup sour cream

1 teaspoon vanilla extract

2 eggs

1. Preheat oven to 350°F. Grease a 9- by 9-inch (23- by 23-cm) baking pan.

2. In a large bowl, mix together the streusel ingredients (cake mix, vanilla extract, oil, and sprinkles). Set aside.

3. In a medium bowl, whisk together the flour, sugar, baking powder, baking soda, and salt.

4. In another bowl, beat the sour cream, vanilla extract, and eggs. Add the dry cake ingredients and combine until moist.

5. Pour batter into prepared baking pan, spreading evenly.

6. Cover batter with crumby streusel. Bake for 40 minutes or until center is set.

CINNAMON ROLLS WITH HONEY GLAZE

From breads to pretzels to rolls, yeast is what turns plain old dough into tasty, lick-your-fingers sweets. Here's a lip-smacking recipe for fluffy, soft cinnamon rolls drizzled with a sweet honey glaze. Waking up never felt so good!

ROLLS

2 teaspoons active dry yeast

1 cup whole milk, warmed to 110°F

1/2 cup granulated sugar

1/4 cup butter, softened

1 teaspoon salt

2 eggs

4 cups all-purpose flour

FILLING

1 cup brown sugar, packed

2 tablespoons cinnamon

1/3 cup butter

1 In a large bowl, dissolve the yeast in the warmed milk. Mix in the sugar, butter, salt, eggs, and flour until totally combined.

2 Cover the bowl in plastic wrap, set in a warm place, and let dough rise for 1 hour or until doubled in size.

3 Meanwhile, in a medium bowl, combine all the filling ingredients and set aside.

4 Preheat oven to 400°F. Grease a pie pan and set aside.

5 On a floured surface, roll out the dough into a rectangle, approximately 0.25 inch (0.5 cm) thick.

6 Using an icing spatula or butter knife, spread the cinnamon-roll filling across the dough evenly.

7 Roll dough lengthwise into a long, cylinder shape. Then cut into 2-inch (5-cm) slices. Place into the pie pan, spacing at least 1.5 inches (4 cm) apart.

8 Bake for 10 minutes or until lightly golden-brown.

GLAZE

1 1/2 cups powdered sugar

3 1/2 tablespoons water

2 tablespoons honey

pinch of salt

TO MAKE

In a small bowl, mix all ingredients to desired thickness.

TO ASSEMBLE

1 Drizzle half of the honey glaze over cinnamon rolls while still hot.

2 Reserve remaining half of honey glaze and drizzle atop individual rolls immediately prior to serving.

MILK BREAD ROLLS AND NEXT–DAY GRIDDLE TOAST

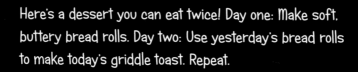

Here's a dessert you can eat twice! Day one: Make soft, buttery bread rolls. Day two: Use yesterday's bread rolls to make today's griddle toast. Repeat.

MILK BREAD ROLLS

1/2 cup granulated sugar

1 tablespoon active dry yeast

2 tablespoons butter

2 cups whole milk

2 teaspoons salt

4 3/4 cups all-purpose flour, separated

1 In a large mixing bowl, combine sugar, yeast, and butter.

2 In a small saucepan, warm milk over medium-low heat until a candy thermometer reaches 110°F. Immediately pour over dry-ingredient mixture. Wait 5 minutes.

3 Add salt and 4 1/2 cups flour. Mix with bread hook for 8 minutes. If you don't have a bread hook, use your hands to knead to the dough.

4 Cover bowl with plastic wrap and set in a warm place. Allow dough to rise approximately an hour or until doubled in size.

5 Place dough on surface covered with 1/4 cup flour and divide into twelve equal pieces.

6 Roll each piece of dough into a smooth ball and place onto a parchment- or Silpat®-lined baking sheet, 2 inches (5 cm) apart.

7 Spray dough balls with nonstick cooking spray or brush with melted butter. Cover with plastic wrap for 30 minutes.

8 Preheat oven to 350°F.

9 Remove plastic wrap. Bake about 20 minutes, turning halfway through. Bread is done when centers are golden and bottoms are golden-brown. Serve hot!

NEXT–DAY GRIDDLE TOAST

day-old milk bread rolls

butter, softened

salt

granulated sugar

1 Slice day-old milk bread rolls in half. Generously butter both sides.

2 Sprinkle lightly with salt and sugar.

3 In a skillet over medium-high heat, cook butter rolls until golden brown.

METRIC CONVERSIONS

The measurements used in this book are imperial units. If you need metric units, check below.

TEMPERATURE

325°F	160°C
350°F	180°C
375°F	190°C
400°F	205°C

VOLUME

1/4 teaspoon	1.25 grams or milliliters
1/2 teaspoon	2.5 g or mL
1 teaspoon	5 g or mL
1 tablespoon	15 g or mL
1/4 cup	57 g (dry) or 60 mL (liquid)
1/3 cup	75 g (dry) or 80 mL (liquid)
1/2 cup	114 g (dry) or 125 mL (liquid)
2/3 cup	150 g (dry) or 160 mL (liquid)
3/4 cup	170 g (dry) or 175 mL (liquid)
1 cup	227 g (dry) or 240 mL (liquid)

READ MORE

Besel, Jen. *Custom Confections: Delicious Desserts You Can Make and Enjoy.* North Mankato, Minn.: Capstone Young Readers, 2015.

Bolte, Mari. *Awesome Recipes You Can Make and Share.* North Mankato, Minn.: Capstone Press, 2015.

Cook, Deanna F. *Baking Class: 50 Fun Recipes Kids Will Love to Bake!* North Adams, Mass.: Storey Publishing, 2017.

Jorgensen, Katrina. *Fearless Food. Allergy-Free Recipes for Kids.* North Mankato, Minn.: Capstone Young Readers, 2017.

INTERNET SITES

Use FactHound to find Internet sites related to this book.

Visit *www.facthound.com*

Just type in 9781543530230 and go.

ABOUT THE AUTHOR

Heather Kim is a pastry chef, painter, and tattoo artist at Minneapolis Tattoo Shop, an all-female owned and operated parlor. Her deliciously unconventional desserts have been praised by the Minneapolis *Star Tribune*, *Minnesota Monthly*, and *Eater*. She lives in Minneapolis with her college sweetheart, Scottie, and their schnauzers, Max and Nietzsche.

Check out all the books in the Sassy Sweets series.

Compass Point Books are published by Capstone
1710 Roe Crest Drive, North Mankato, Minnesota 56003
www.mycapstone.com

Image Credits
Photographs by Capstone Studio: Karon Dubke, except: Shutterstock: AnnapolisStudios, 36 Inset, Arayabandit, 6 Bottom Left, atdr, 4 Bottom Left, Becky Starsmore, 7 Bottom, DONOT6_STUDIO, 43, Elena P, 36 Background, M. Unal Ozmen, 6 Top Right, Michal Schwarz, 4 Middle Left, VictorH11, 6 Top Left, wavebreakmedia, 4 Top Left, Yuliya Gontar, Design Element, 4-5, 46-47

Editorial Credits
Abby Colich, editor; Juliette Peters and Charmaine Whitman, designers; Tracy Cummins, media researcher; Laura Manthe, production specialist

Library of Congress Cataloging-in-Publication Data
Names: Kim, Heather, 1978- author.
Title: I donut dare you! : bold breakfast-inspired desserts for anytime / by Heather Kim.
Description: North Mankato, Minnesota : Compass Point Books, a Capstone Imprint, [2019] | Series: Sassy sweets | Audience: Age 9-11. | Audience: Grade 4 to 6. | Includes bibliographical references.
Identifiers: LCCN 2018017829| ISBN 9781543530230 (library binding) | ISBN 9781543530285 (ebook pdf)
Subjects: LCSH: Desserts. | LCGFT: Cookbooks.
Classification: LCC TX773 .K525 2019 | DDC 641.86—dc23
LC record available at https://lccn.loc.gov/2018017829

Printed in the United States of America.
PA021